Kimmy Joy

Mattress Dungeon

2021 ♦ Grand Rapids

*for Charis,
may your gifts be
a blessing, not a weight.*

© 2021 by Kimmy Joy.

FIRST EDITION.

This book uses two typefaces: Minion 3, designed by Robert Slimbach, and for the headings, New Spirit, designed by Miles Newlyn and Riccardo Olocco.

Cover design by Ian McDonough.
Interior design by Christopher McCaffery.

When I started my blog, *Mattress Dungeon*, I'd only been writing poetry for about three months. I'd written lots of poems as a child and had dreams of becoming a rich and famous poet. These dreams were crushed when I was sixteen and went off to poetry camp for a month, where I learned that not only do poets typically die in obscurity, I was the worst poet in my group. I shifted focus and decided to write songs instead, and then I wrote plays, and then I fell into a deep depression and wrote nothing. I started writing poetry again out of a life-or-death need to be writing something, anything, even if it wasn't any good, even if nobody was really reading it. Thus, *Mattress Dungeon* was born.

It's awkward thinking of putting this collection out into the world in a form other than an anonymous blog. To me, writing a poem feels like telling a secret—I can bury it in layers of wordplay or obscure it with abstraction, but generally if I'm writing a poem, it's because I'm thinking or feeling something that I don't think I can tell anyone. In a way, though, that's a blessing. I don't feel the need to really self-promote or try to publish these poems in any form other than just sticking them between two covers. The insecurity and vulnerability that comes with telling secrets lends itself nicely to creating an artifact that will most likely stay under the radar of, say, major publishers, and by way of that invisibility, my mom.

I've still got that "worst poet at poetry camp" fear. If you read this collection and enjoy even just one poem, that's a win in my book. And this is my book, so hopefully there's a win in here somewhere.

table of contents

to anyone interested	2
two out of three	4
nocturne: swamp thing	6
should've been us	8
blank speech	10
angel from that one place	12
cassavetes pt ii	14
truth or time or bodies or enlightenment or awareness or	16
lonesome and ready	18
lock your own door, pt. ii	20
it hasn't been my day for a couple years	22
filament	24
venomous progression	26
what i was trying to say was	28
reverse dutch boy	30
i barely know 'er	32
run tell blake	34
he's gonna start a war	36
reasons for leaving your senses	38
we could be mirrors	40
the secret languages have no textbook	42
words as gas as trees as words	44
nocturne: the sea appears at a certain depth	46
compared to all the local celebrities	48
waning crescent	50
cassavetes says he isn't taking my calls anymore	52
patience pending	54
five excuses	56
i never dream about the mountains	58
the eternal living room	60
by the river, by the street	62

mattress dungeon: poems

to anyone interested

my feet look like they're carved
from marble the veins
outstanding long slender
toes smooth unencumbered
free of heavy boots wool socks
blandly pretty nothing special maybe
i could get around some other way
if i pass my driver's test in july

it's been so hard though i swear
working feels like dying some days
and we both slept better before all the deaths
but he shakes in his sleep
these gasping jolts and jerks
i pull away i roll over i hug a pillow
it's nothing sane or fair
but lord i miss the peace of dreaming
while touching
this digital rain washes nothing clean

and under all of it the anger
you've heard it all before so
i will spare you, mostly, and say
the joy has fled like everything i loved
was a drug that's lost its buzz
chasing maintenance doses of happiness
this dragon burns pitifully under my tongue

the words in my head have been caged
and grown claws to scratch and throats to cry
good morning they say will you spend some time
with us today oh we so long to escape
and find another to caress to lick to kiss
i mumble an apology into my coffee cup
it's not a good time i say
never a good time, never anymore

i hurt from crown to arch
so anyway
it'll be fifty bucks for a couple photos

two out of three

in the beginning was the word
quickened fluttering in the stomach
given breath and born
into its shape in your mouth
we handle this verbal clay
with varying levels of grace
i missed your mastery of sculpture
the voluptuous, luscious L
like slow-dripped honey
the uh a rounded bubble
rising with its soft throaty thrust
the V carved sharp
by teeth against lip
smudged edge of lush forest
on the warm sweet smell of tongue
an opioid blanket bearing velvet
down the spine and into the core
bruised fruit plucked from stem
and handed fresh to me
no wonder
i always bit deep

nocturne: swamp thing

something about standing
in a swamp slimed with pond scum
building a bridge with fallen trees
surprised at what i can carry
these strangers approach
calling me by name
they have a letter for me
mistakenly delivered years ago
when it would have mattered
the envelope is covered with
notes about how to find me
they've made it a mystery to solve
they seem so proud

my family has crossed the bridge
i am alone in the muck
with a silver bowl of fresh water
and the letter, flavorless with age
he writes to give a detailed update
his creative process is going well
he has borrowed poems
from his brother's friends
in the care home in iowa
he has enclosed some photos
you should really try this keyboard

the strangers watch me
take off my clothes
and splash silver water
on my face and hair and shoulders
i can't feel anything
about his words
i wish i had walked
across my wooden bridge

you know what i love about museums
sometimes they burn all the way down

should've been us

the part that rips me apart
is you play a tough guy on tv
gunslinger with soft hands
that betray the lie in every touch
oh you're such a character
i wonder sometimes
if i molded you out of my own
synapses and neurons
and quickened heartbeats

blank speech

well because see i have this thing with wanting
i wasn't allowed to want things when i was a kid
the heart is deceitful above all things
and desperately wicked
who can know it
hot damn sometimes
the bible contains really great poetry
i was always a psalms girl myself
yeah that and ezekiel
yearning for deliverance from yearning

like i'll have moments where i know i should be alone
and silent and rest and read books
and i'll say yes anyway and push back pain
and fatigue and irritation
and go out with people and drink
and i'll do this for weeks and weeks and
and one day i find myself hating everyone
and wanting to run away

yeah okay you get it. and it's like that
with love too like i'll be in denial about a
fucking crush for days weeks months
until what the fuck that's not a crush
that's an obsession my good bitch

oh and the capacity for obsession, god
that's a whole nother story
i've got too much free
time to obsess obsess obsess
and not enough to express
how it feels from the inside
of course i keep trying
nature of the beast i guess
at this point i've grown
used to the embarrassment
like bad hiccups in public

so yeah you guessed it
i've been drinking because drinking
(somehow) is an ok thing
to want
every single day round these parts
i'm starting to think i'll never feel free
in a city with so many bars
supporting the brunch-industrial complex
it's also ok as a method of self-punishment
i'll get blitzed enough that i don't have to finish my

angel from that one place

i guess i should have guessed
how the light would catch your eyes
& how quick how strong
the fever would set in
seatbelts off in this reckless wreck
burned alive in the chill wind
off the lake where you wrapped me up
& the room where you slapped me up
& how i would feel so trapped
at the loud ringing distance
don't get me wrong i've walked further
but tonight there's glass in my feet
& i can't stop shaking baby i
can't tell you how sorry i am

we have all kinds of reasons for choosing
numbness or joy or pain
dashing helter skelter into rough waters
but in an emergency it's easier
to forget this trait is shared
& written into our dna
it is easier to hide out of shame
to pretend you're the only one
who wanted to bodysurf at high tide
i got no way to predict or explain

place your palm against my cheek
you may choose
the delicacy of its landing

cassavetes pt ii

suicidal instinct can manifest
in one's choice of partner
we push each other out of line
and hope to make chalk lines
out of these piles of snow

when he says: let's drink and drive
i spring for the 12% abv
when the road twists ahead
my laugh echoes off the shale walls
i know which songs to play
to make him push the pedal harder

in the living room it's drugs and guns
in the bedroom it's hands around throat
in the bone room housing my thoughts
it's a prayer for ultimate release
from loss
from need

i tried to be good with you
and bad with him
but you were a rock
and i wanted a blade

like i said
these girls they love a bad boy
these girls they crave and beg the lie
you got this starring role, kid
your death scene will sweep the Oscars

we all love the ones
who let us see them bleed
we love the loss
we hate the need

when the waves crash
when the hurricane comes
god it hurts so bad
to cling to a boulder
beaten by the surf
with little hope of rescue

i looked at you and saw a certain
hope i hope to hope for me
i looked at him and saw
the same loss
the same need
perhaps you can't believe

but i always held you dearer
still: one can smash a mirror
make a blade to make it clearer

the sharp turns up on the mountain
felt like a kind of salvation
show me grace
if i ever try to fly like this again

truth or time or bodies or enlightenment or awareness or

my love are you still
breathing in the depths
somewhere in my spirit
i have missed our talks
under water dark as ice
just a short swim away
from the city of lights
i never got to visit

you told me if i left that day
i would never be able to return
and there were so many people
waiting to meet me down below
my love is that where i will go
when i fall asleep for the last time
is that what you meant
i didn't want to leave

this vague distance drowns me
too many times i linger
on the thought of what you'd say
to all this mess to me as I am
i wonder if you'd be proud of me
i wonder if you are proud of me

my love i am dying of thirst
please tell me one more time
what we're talking about
when we talk about water

lonesome and ready

how dare you send me west
toward the mountains
installing your wistful dreams
like so much software
i may be a city girl
but i can drive hard
& i can climb

how to love someone:
learn them & outshine them
they'll certainly be impressed
(this actually never works
but i've never read a map
better suited for)
expressing & navigating
the territory of total adoration

but here the terrain
outpaces me &
this cinderblock
box of comfort
cannot hold me
back oh hold me
back oh hold me

back in the olden days
facedown in the dirt
with a blow to the head i dreamed
flight & the city's wilderness light
a tense conjugal prayer:
stars flew stars fly stars fall
i flew i fly i fall
i rose i rise i raise
flat on my back i
surfaced
i breathed i breathe
i breathe i breathe

i fled to weaker arms
i flee to strong shoulders
i'll fly to the mountain & climb
tirelessly on bleeding feet
without outpacing
& sleep in the trees
below: your shrine
an aluminum casket
above: granite, pink quartz
& stars flying
& stars falling
& we fly
& we fall

lock your own door, pt. ii

should i switch to tequila
in spite of our rotten limes
feet in lead boots
roll me into the river
watch me sink
in defiance of your expectations
oh you thought i'd fight
you thought i'd swim
you did did you
sorry to disappoint
but what's else is new

my patience is as short
as your memory
or your attention span
or the straw i drew
down on you in my dreams
and you flinched but
lied about it later you said
you love being a target

that cognitive dissonance
is so sweet as a shield
the deviance your decisions
make for you entwined
in the map dad wrote you
as an infant in your early twenties
holding your bottle

of cheap beer and cheaper laughs
we were born free
and spend our lives
decorating prisons

i see your open window
i've flown some myself
you talk like you know
that i can't keep up
like it's not worth trying
like the breath you'll breathe outside
will be sweeter
and it will
i won't argue that

but it hollows out the other thing
and leaves me empty after injection
after injection when i have
this problem where i have
to take matters into my own hands
love is a word you use defensively
so much is a null compared to nothing

you have no stakes
but oh aren't you the prettiest
room in the world

it hasn't been my day for a couple years

a partial list of sins &
character defects: i
have this thing for blasphemy
i love the smell of money
i'm highly susceptible to boredom
and leather
and coercion
and shoplifting

i like hurting people
but i hate it when they cry
take it like a man, man
blood tastes better than tears

i have a gnawing hungry fetish
for unattainability
at any given moment
i'm in love with two (2) people
that i can't have

i like control
i want control
when i get control
i want to give up control
and be controlled

like a shining substance
in a lustful glass vial
to be consumed

i hate
that manic pixie airhead bimbo shit
right up until i'm Wanted
& then i'm painting my eyelashes
to improve my batting average

i think i'm smarter than i am
i think i'm stupid

my heart is an anvil
i want to forge you into steel
and you are made of glass
and in a way i'm not sorry at all

when i die
make sure my tombstone reads:
devoted friend
shameless flirt

filament

there is a kind of nameless bliss
descending in these quiet moments
so what if it comes with pain
we've never been strangers to each other
it's proof in its own way
that the universe doesn't owe me sense
or coincidence
and it's even lovelier watching things fade

this is a sunset on a shopping mall
this is a crumbled pillar in a park
this isn't that one guy, alone
in his bedroom with a single light shining
i was there, you know
in the filament, powerless
breathing him in the dark
it almost killed me too
but by then i knew
how to take a hit

& so did he, i guess
funny hilarious how we play out
these scripts we wrote
before the world began
time is a womb & the pain
just means we're being born again
all of us, together

i'm here, i'm here in your blood
& your breath & the filament

venomous progression

the snake coiled in my gut
has the typical markings
of a Midwestern Heartbreaker
filthy isolation & yearning
no appetite & poor sleep
the mind running over & over
words spoken & unspoken
the extra muscle it takes
to pick up a pen & write
the same trite bullshit
as everyone else who's had a bite

take me to a bank
with a robbery in progress
i'll throw myself at the thieves
maybe steal a gun
i'd rather blow my brains out
than eat cheese & crackers again
my wrist looks tender enough
to bite through
with very little effort

people of earth, rejoice
with handles of molson
& cases of labatt
ain't nobody gonna cry tonight
i'm dry as a fucking bone
i've just got the classic symptoms, see
you've got me or you got me
or i'm free

what i was trying to say was

creatively barren times
lead to bad decisions
i have thrown a sledgehammer
at my values system
and watched it shatter like ice
only men enter my house now
and i can't bring myself
to love any of them

oh trust is such a hard thing
for a shackled heart
and a mind full of rusty nails
i am diving back into a lake of pages
hoping for hope and finding
it's all variations on a theme

love and lust and lots of loss
we could chant this mantra
until the sun burns out
knowing these things full well
and still unbelieving
receiving these painful gifts
at a surprise party we threw ourselves

reverse dutch boy

the river of my desire
once seemed to flood & drown
every good thing i had
so i built a strong dam
& let myself take small sips
from the lake that grew
year by year

he took a sledgehammer
& relentlessly swung &
hacked giant holes
through concrete & rebar
stood firm in the rush
laughing as it soaked him
he said, there. you're free.
& then he left

i could be angry at the absence
or i could thank him
for his strong tools
& his steady arms
but mostly
it just hurts to want again
i have no idea what to do
with all of this water

i barely know 'er

from my vantage point behind the desk
i can see rib fragments and detached limbs
and brain matter and dark bloody muscle
stretched out mosaic on the concrete
the stomach twists and writhes
the heart hovers, moaning hummingbird
i want to mash all the pieces together
form them into something that'll live
but seeing how the bones scrape slow
freezes my soul motionless

you phased through the flesh
fist grips trachea
your timepiece is broken
and i'm begging you
to lay off the penetrating conversation
can't we just laugh like we used to
can't we just
ain't we just the most grotesque
when we're trying
i'm gonna buy you a calendar
i'm gonna buy you a drink
i'm gonna buy you a new set of internal organs
i'm gonna buy you

as far as the black market goes
i predict an uptick in the supply
of anxiety poems
with body horror imagery
my google search:
"poets who died of spanish flu"
returned nobody of note
guess that's the way it always is
historically we drink
enough that it always comes back
to the liver
and i'm particularly good
at living

i am so unfamiliar with this
pile of shredded meat at my feet
i can't really tell how much
the ethanol affected the yes/no
dichotomy
it's a whole weird thing i say
and i can't locate the liver
the liver, the liver where's the liver
where's the part that's still alive

why did i let you push
that knife into me
so many times

run tell blake

anyway i was listening to jets to brazil
when my sister told me
that our dad was gonna die
i couldn't leave work
and i didn't have a grand on hand
to buy a last-minute ticket to miami
what a horrible place to die
after an expensive air ambulance ride
might as well stay home
and let your body nourish
the land you actually love

anyway perfecting loneliness hit different
and rocket boy tore a hole in my heart
projectile weeping next to the ovens
flames evaporating my tears
i've got a tattoo of that moment
on my left ventricle
they'll see it when they cut me open
at age 63 because i inherited
dad's heart and habits
and i never take my lisinopril
but to be fair i rarely get angry

anyway dad lived to tell more tall tales
and now he's stuck in florida again
but i guess that's okay
he always hated it here

he's gonna start a war

fresh blood, fresh snow
sent screaming sober
dancing without drinking
is not the usual in this town
we cowboys are all desperate
for a new war or a new frontier
the plains are cold tonight
and we ride
sore hearts and eyes
searching for the last wild buffalo
it'll look so good on instagram
i've got the filter picked out already
something good for low light
god it's so dark out here
it's so fucking dark out here

you can develop an immunity
to homesickness if you move fast enough
the hard part is slowing down
home is in the motion, the speed
sitting still you feel the fire
ants crawling over your soul
in the silence
you try to make out
the polychord of your tinnitus

no wonder we keep it loud
no wonder we drink to stay awake
no wonder we ride hard past dawn
and keep the guns strapped tight
no wonder we kiss strangers
no wonder we cry out; the sun goes quiet
we must have a song, darling
hand me that harmonica
and sing it one more time

reasons for leaving your senses

the hot wind of frustration
meets the cold front of isolation
a hurricane builds on the horizon
it calls itself by your secret name

evacuation plans torn by wind
from their sweaty hands
the small people on the shore
grip beach sand with their toes

whatever it is that keeps them
holding to a home that is already lost
bravery or idiocy or blind stunned fear
is certainly notable

we could be mirrors

you know what it is
to starve on a full stomach
to walk in cold rain
like you can wash the words loose
like your sore feet will write for you
& you know what it is to implode

tonight only the dirt's visible
there are condoms & needles in my driveway
both used & i used to laugh
there's another —
another sad symbol
tonight i just wanna kill that guy
the one across the alley
who leaves his dogs caged outside

see it's cold & i know you know
& i'm sorry but some nights
this music just makes me
just makes me want to bleed
as melodramatically as possible

from the mouth, maybe,
from the stomach
because i can't — won't stop eating
hey, maybe you don't know.
but the words are out there,
somewhere. gimme.

the secret languages have no textbook

for Mike Doughty

have you learned by now
that the twists and grooves
of a certain mindshape
slip gently into abstract curls
of language, of melody
of voice

when they elaborate at length
you saved my life in 2007
so graceless, your grace
you must know
the liquid tangles of wiring
pore over your metaphor
to find an opening

the shock of recognition
tines connecting
to twinned plastic orifices
this electricity bends to addiction
addiction to displacement
they find their home
on a map you drew

sound the alarm at planted flags
of course your inner self
is your most valuable possession
these blackeyed slackjawed grins
beg to claim as their own
clamoring for a slice of soul
as if they'd take your skin
if they just had a knife

there was a time when i fell
and fell into the kind of dark
where a good old na na na
splits the life/death difference
but our hearts grow and learn
forgive me
you knew not what you said

here — a shoebox taped shut firm
and wildly addressed to the void
contents: all the pieces
i once tried to take
returned, with my regrets
i have no claim to stake

words as gas
as trees as words

there's probably an extended metaphor
about a car that can go fast as hell
and no doubt for long distances
if you don't mind the constant presence
of alert lights and the frequent danger
of getting pulled over with no license
but the diminishing returns have hit
and my whole thing right now is
you won't speak clearly
there's always some part breaking down
and you send me under the hood
over and over to diagnose
and replace broken things
and you've got me back in the metaphor
because it's a vulnerable thing
admitting you're off balance
and i know part of you wants me to beg
to see how far you can push me
before i take off my seat belt
and hit the gas as hard as i can
but i know you've got a brick wall
all planned out and built
and baby i love you
but i ain't driving drunk tonight
and i'm back in the fucking metaphor
goddamnit

nocturne: the sea appears at a certain depth

language practice
in a grimy diner
laughing at gibberish
she followed me out
to film the parking lot
aspin behind the camera
i joined the dancers
dizzy with cobblestones
cutting our feet bloody
i caught branches to swing
in the soft grey damp
floating upward becomes natural
if you let go of gravity
a simple matter of pointing
head as compass and engine
to rocket into the blue
three layers of rush and zoom
past mandalas of cloud
to the inverted Sea above
i paused hovering
a vertical straight line
vibrating as you taught me
knowing if i broke the surface
you'd be there waiting
and i cried out your name
as my head touched the water
i crowned with a yelp
into consciousness
in which universe do i find myself
this time around

compared to all the local celebrities

this box of brains
feels so much less
than special at times
wishing that my favorite
artists weren't so uncool
or that i cared about houseplants
and had an eye for decorating
or a gender identity
or that i played tennis really well
that languages would stick
and i could cite theory
while i give you a glimpse
of the horsehead nebula
through my elaborate telescope
before utterly blowing your mind
in lingerie, size six, 34D
this is a shallow desire
for a shallow life
faced with all this
who's gonna care
that i used to play the guitar ok
that i make pretty good soup
i can define dactylic tetrameter
and understand when you talk
about the difficulties of personhood
who's gonna care
who's gonna care
i mean
i can't even make myself care

waning crescent

back when you held the concept
of unquestionably wrong
before love contorted itself
and your methods went sharp
before your taste of heaven
sent you downwards
the cold cold ground lumping up
saying i will meet you son
you always belonged to me

relentless against the nascent day
did you stand mudspattered
did you call your resistance a curse
returning weary and empty
which twist in the wire
was the one to send you spinning

what we choose to memorialize
controls us in its way
i remember you as the moon
lifting soft and bright
some small gift
in the curve and shine
of your shoulders bent
over that other light

cassavetes says he isn't taking my calls anymore

suppose there's a point of pointlessness
where complaining just puts you in
one of those obligating positions
and low-maintenance seems best
but lo it is lonely waiting again
bitches i'm back to having
nothing but some bit part
of someone else's lowlife

hearts want what hearts want
what hearts want what hearts
want what hearts want what
heart wants the consolation kiss
which creates no difference
between you and i
whatever is in my body
now lives in your body
so what offense
has my body caused
besides damselhood

your personal villain comes
with you wherever you go
whatever is in my body
now lives in his body
his offenses are many
he will be greeted warmly

these girls they love a bad boy
these girls they crave and beg the lie
these girls have become addicted
to filters on their photographs
and nail polish and lipstick
so they cain't hardly look
in the mirror without a soft cringe
these girls they would do anything
for someone who says the kinds of words
that have existed only as
imagined intonations

you understand yes
that center frame is irresistible
even momentarily
these girls they need an agent
and a casting director
who will fight for them
to win a leading role

someone tell these girls
they need new headshots

patience pending

darling if you're going to tell stories
you must first establish a firm timeline
and a coherent series of events
you see i've read some very fine literature
written drunk and edited hungover
i have high standards for tall tales
you can bring me low and short me
but don't try to sell me something
unworthy of publication

five excuses

I. hollow voice to empty ears

because i shot words
like bullets to the black night
singing the meteor shower
cat-clawing until the notes shattered
and fell spent and sweating
at the feet of a mumbling crowd
who don't seem to like purple
nearly as much as i do

II. smash cut: age eight

because she used to say
when you write your bestseller
instead of if
the expectation a seed
to a tree to a fruit too big
too ripe too rotten
to hope for anything
except that it might seed again

III. zero style points

because my attention span leads to inconsistency
leads to the sort of shaky artistry that makes
it difficult to convince myself that anything
worthwhile can come out of the sort of stream of
conscious bitterness that tends to plague me and i
want to write something that accomplishes a goal
further than making hostile eye contact with the
reader while i take all of my clothes off and smear a
thin coat of paint on my skin without telling a single
goddamn joke to break the tension

IV. what if you're wrong

because a calling supposedly has a flavor
that is more easily tasted from the outside
so easy to condescend and call it
ego or arrogance or attention-seeking
and is it not ego to say
i know myself better than you do
is it not arrogance to say i was born for this
is it not attention-seeking to say
i have something good inside of me
if i am wrong i am undone

V. the rent is always due

because there's an injured sparrow
shaking terrified in my hands
and if i set it aside it will die
and i have this knowledge
at every moment

i never dream
about the mountains

might be there's a lesson
about choosing to move forward
walking on blisters
trundling forward
on nothing but the sheer hope
that there's an oasis
in the next mile

strange to think we loved each other
in interesting times
that if we all survive this
the memory will be infected
with the ones who were the closest

strap on the time helmet
take me back to the moment
we first spoke and i knew
something about you something
important my mind and heart
stumbled for a moment who
is that why did the record skiptell me the story then and
see
how well i believe you
love is not an easy thing
to understand love
is not an easy thing

here i am with the blisters
here i am

the eternal living room

if i ever meet god i want to ask it
why people seem to hurt me
when i've been actively straining
toward kindness
and why i was born
with such a sense
of the importance of everyone else
if this messiah complex
has any sort of purpose
and why one little slight
sends me sailing off
on a rough sick sea of self hatred
and will i ever get over this

and god would be like
damn bitch
those are some pretty uh
self involved questions

oh, uh
doesn't everyone want to know
this sort of personal insight stuff
i figured that'd be pretty common

nah, says god
most people ask me about
like idk black holes
and deja vu and shit
or who killed kennedy
i get that one a lot
oh and aliens
everyone always asks
about the fucking aliens
i notice you didn't
i guess that's refreshing

yeah, sorry, i
was kind of in a mood
the night i came up with
all these questions
maybe i should have revised them

god mutes the tv
look, it says, you know the answers
to every question you just asked me
you just don't like the answers
and you wanted someone
you could whine to
deal with your shit
get a therapist
this isn't fucking cosmic

i feel pretty ashamed
but obviously i don't want god to see
but it's god
so it totally does
i just kinda shift around
and finally say
ok so tell me about the aliens

oh so now you care about
the me-damn aliens, huh
you'll find out about them
soon enough
now go call that therapist
i'm trying to watch breaking bad

by the river, by the street

i think you'd love me most
in small moments of perseverance
carrying the groceries home
slipping in the snow
i grasp desperately
for the heart shadowing mine
and hope that your firm grasp
will keep me standing

you are a counterweight
a balance a nightlight
a cup of strong coffee
a sleeping pill if needed
remember this

i think you'd love me most
if i never had to tell you anything
and existed whole inside you
built out of bricks and steel
you could lean and sag against me
in moments of fatigue

i have so much to tell you
i have so much to say
i have so much wonder
i am so tired

when i lie down
you dream with me

about the author

Kimmy Joy is the founder and lead producer of The Brutal Sea, an art collective focused on experimental theatre in Grand Rapids, Michigan. This is her first collection of poetry.

You can email Kimmy at musicalchairs@gmail.com.

Deepest gratitude to Dave, Dex, Dusty, Jon, Chris, Ian, Leah, Gillian, Bruce, and Jared for everything from inspiration and encouragement to shelter during the early pandemic (and the early stages of this project).